Firefighter

Firefighter

Kathleen Ermitage

A Harcourt Company

Austin   New York
www.steck-vaughn.com

Copyright © 2000, Steck-Vaughn Company

All rights reserved. No part of this book may be reproduced or utilized in any form or by any means, electronic or mechanical, including photocopying, recording, or by any information storage and retrieval system, without permission in writing from the Publisher. Inquiries should be addressed to: Copyright Permissions, Steck-Vaughn Company, P.O. Box 26015, Austin, TX 78755.

Published by Raintree Steck-Vaughn Publishers,
an imprint of Steck-Vaughn Company

Art Director: Max Brinkmann
Editor: Pam Wells
Design and Illustration: Proof Positive/Farrowlyne Associates, Inc.
Planned and Produced by
Proof Positive/Farrowlyne Associates, Inc.

Library of Congress Cataloging-in-Publication Data

Ermitage, Kathleen.
   Firefighter/Kathleen Ermitage.
     p. cm. — (Workers you know)
   Summary: Describes the many aspects of a firefighter's job and the training and skills needed in this important profession.
   ISBN 0-8172-5597-4
    1. Fire extinction—Vocational guidance—Juvenile literature. 2. Fire prevention—Juvenile literature. 3. Fire fighters—Juvenile literature. [1. Fire fighters. 2. Occupations.] I. Title. II. Series.

TH9148 .E76 2000
628.9'25—dc21

99-054426

Printed and bound in the United States
1 2 3 4 5 6 7 8 9 0 LB 03 02 01 00

Acknowledgments:
Photo Credits: **15:** © David Joe/Tony Stone Images

Note: You will find more information about becoming a firefighter on the last page of this book.

Do you like helping people? For many workers, helping people is just part of the job. You could become a doctor or nurse. You could become a teacher. Or you could become a rescue worker.

Paramedics give first aid to people at the scene of an accident. Police officers help people in all kinds of emergencies. And firefighters—people like me—rescue people from fires and put the fires out.

My name is Mike Miller. It is 5:00 A.M. The fire alarm is ringing! I jump out of bed and put on my work clothes. It only takes me a few seconds to get dressed. When the fire alarm goes off, a firefighter has no time to waste.

Soon after the fire alarm rings, I climb onto the fire truck. The rest of the team is there already. As we speed to the fire's location, I turn on the truck's bright lights and sirens. Because we're moving quickly, we need to warn the other drivers so they know we're coming. Cars and trucks pull over to the side of the road in order to give me a clear path to drive through.

Before we left for the fire, we created a plan of action. Firefighters can't waste time talking while a building is burning down, so we plan ahead. We divide up into groups, called companies. Each company has a different job to do. My company's job is to make sure all the people are safe. Lamont, the fire captain in charge of my company, leads us as we race into the building.

The temperature in a burning building can be as high as 1500 degrees Fahrenheit. We wear special clothes to protect us. Our coats and pants are made of special cloth that doesn't catch fire as easily as regular cloth. Our boots and gloves protect us from flames, water, and other dangerous things. The helmets protect our heads from falling objects.

Even with the special clothes we wear, firefighting is dangerous. When a building is burning, floors and walls sometimes collapse. Sometimes parts of the building explode. That's why only a trained firefighter should enter a burning building.

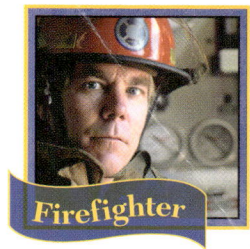

Firefighter

Inside, the building is filled with smoke. Smoke is one of the things that makes a fire so dangerous. Breathing smoke can make someone pass out. So we switch on our air tanks to help us breathe. We have 30 minutes worth of air in our tanks.

We go through every room in the building to make sure everyone got out. If a door is locked, we have to break it down. We have special tools we can use to rescue people who are trapped. We also have rescue airbags and a ventilator (**ven**-till-ate-ter)— tools we can use to help people breathe.

While we search for people, the other companies are doing other jobs. One company connects a special fire truck called a pumper to a fire hydrant. The pumper takes water from the hydrant and shoots it through a hose. In one minute, a pumper pumps out more than 1,000 gallons of water! It takes time to hook up the pumper, so the fire truck carries 500 gallons of water along with it—enough to start putting the fire out before the pumper is hooked up. In this way, the company can begin to fight the fire immediately.

Are you wondering why it takes so many people to spray the fire with a hose? The water comes through the hose so fast that the pressure makes it hard to control the hose. It takes several strong firefighters to hold the hose still and point it in the direction of the fire.

For this fire, water was all that was needed, but we don't always use water to put out a fire. Sometimes we use foam, a chemical spray that looks like soapsuds. Foam can put out fires that are burning in liquids, like oil. Foam can also get to areas that are hard to reach.

Even after we think the fire is out, we have to make sure. We check every room and every corner in the building. We look for anything that could possibly start the fire again.

Nancy Alvarez

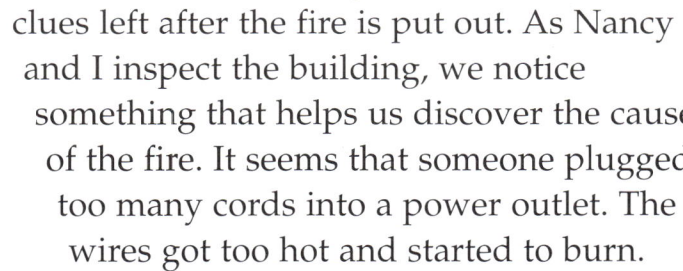

Nancy Alvarez is the fire marshal. Like most fire marshals, she's more of a detective. She tries to figure out how a fire got started from the clues left after the fire is put out. As Nancy and I inspect the building, we notice something that helps us discover the cause of the fire. It seems that someone plugged too many cords into a power outlet. The wires got too hot and started to burn.

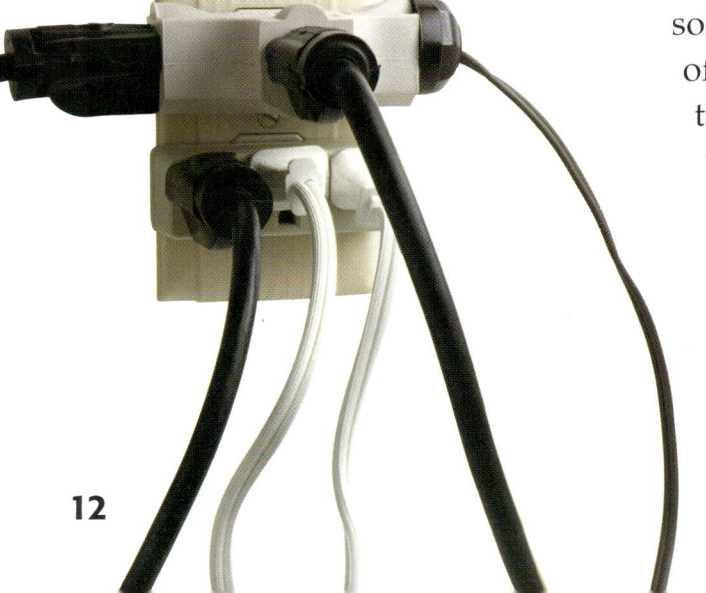

When we're not fighting fires, we check all of our equipment. We make sure everything works perfectly. If any parts are broken or cracked, we replace them. We oil the equipment to make sure all the parts can move smoothly. We also dry out the water hoses.

It's my job to check the air tanks. I look for any leaks in the breathing masks or tanks. I also replace the empty tanks with full ones.

It's also my job to check the two-way radio on our fire truck. We need to speak clearly to headquarters. When we're at a fire, we let them know what we find. That way, if we need more help, the dispatcher can radio other firefighters and rescue workers to come to the scene of the fire. "To dispatch" means to send something very fast.

Firefighters go to school for two years to learn about fire fighting. We learn what causes a fire and how fires travel. We learn what different buildings are made of, and what can happen if they catch fire. Our teachers make sure we know how water pressure changes when water rushes through a hose and nozzle. Most of what we learn is science, but we also practice sharing information with other people by talking, listening, and writing. I have been a firefighter for 15 years, but I am still learning.

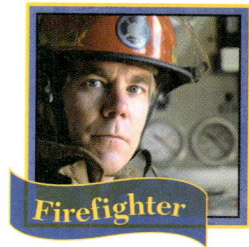
Firefighter

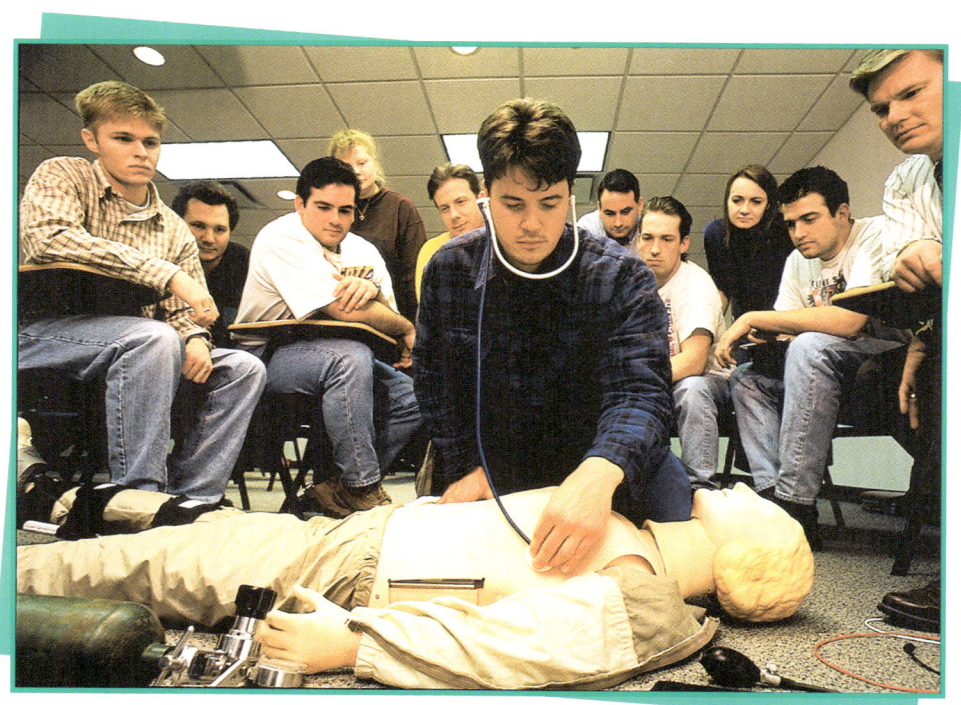

15

Firefighters need to be healthy and strong. Some of the hoses we use weigh more than one hundred pounds! We also need to be able to run up stairs quickly. Before we can be firefighters, we are tested on our strength and quickness.

For one test we have to carry 50 pounds of hose up several flights of stairs. For another we have to drag a 150-pound dummy for 100 feet, to find out if we are strong enough to pull people out of a fire. In one test I had to climb over a wall that was eight feet tall!

Does your school ever have fire drills? Firefighters have drills, too. In this drill, I am practicing using a ladder truck with Monica, a new firefighter. A ladder truck helps firefighters rescue people in tall buildings. We also use ladder trucks to bring water hoses to the upper stories of a building. Some ladder trucks reach up to eight stories high.

Monica and I will practice putting up this ladder and climbing to the top again and again. We want to be able to climb the ladder without even thinking about it. Then, we'll go inside and practice first aid and CPR. First aid is emergency medical help, like treating a burn or a cut. CPR is a way to help people if they stop breathing or if their hearts stop beating. Firefighters have to be ready to help people who get hurt in a fire.

Monica

Firefighters don't always put fires out. Sometimes, we can stop fires before they begin. My friend Bruce is a fire inspector.

His job is to check people's homes for fire hazards, which are possible sources of fire. Today, I helped him to inspect a friend's home.

We looked for anything that could start a fire. We looked for trash, chemicals, and other materials that burn easily. Bruce and I checked all the wires to make sure they had plastic coating. Then, we inspected all the smoke alarms to make sure they were working. Finally, we checked the exits and fire escapes. Luckily, we didn't find any fire hazards, but we did replace a battery in a smoke alarm.

Firefighter

Are there any fire risks where you live? Look at these pictures of fire risks. Then, check your home. If you can find any of these risks, you should tell a grown-up. By checking your home for things that might cause fires, you make my job a lot easier.

19

Sandy and Paul are part of a special club called Young Firefighters. My fire station started the club to teach kids about fire safety. Every week, kids from our town come to the fire station. We talk about how fires start. We also talk about what you should do in case of a fire.

future firefighters

Firefighter

Today I talked to the club about what causes fires. Why do fires start? The science of chemistry can explain it. First, there must be a material that can catch on fire easily. The temperature must get hot enough to start a fire. And there must be enough oxygen in the air to help the fire burn.

Sometimes fires start when a burning match or candle falls onto a rug. But other times fires start on their own. Think about a pile of oily rags sitting in a closet. The oil in the rags combines with oxygen in the air to give off heat. If the heat is trapped—in a closet, for example—there is no moving air to carry the heat away. If the chemicals in the rags get hot enough, they can burst into flames—even if nobody ever lights a match.

Firefighter

After the club meeting, it's time for me to do some chores. Firefighters spend so much time at the fire station that it's like our home. We work here 50 or 60 hours a week, and our shifts can last for 24 hours at a time. We also do chores here at the firehouse, just like you do chores at your home. We do things like mowing the lawn and sweeping.

We take turns doing the chores at the fire station. Sometimes I buy groceries. Sometimes I do the laundry. Sometimes we exercise or play basketball to stay in shape.

Tonight it was my turn to make dinner. I made chili. All the firefighters are happy when it is my turn to make dinner. They love my chili.

You never know when the fire alarm is going to ring. But whenever it rings—even if I'm just sitting down to dinner—I have to be ready to go. When someone is in danger, I want to help them.

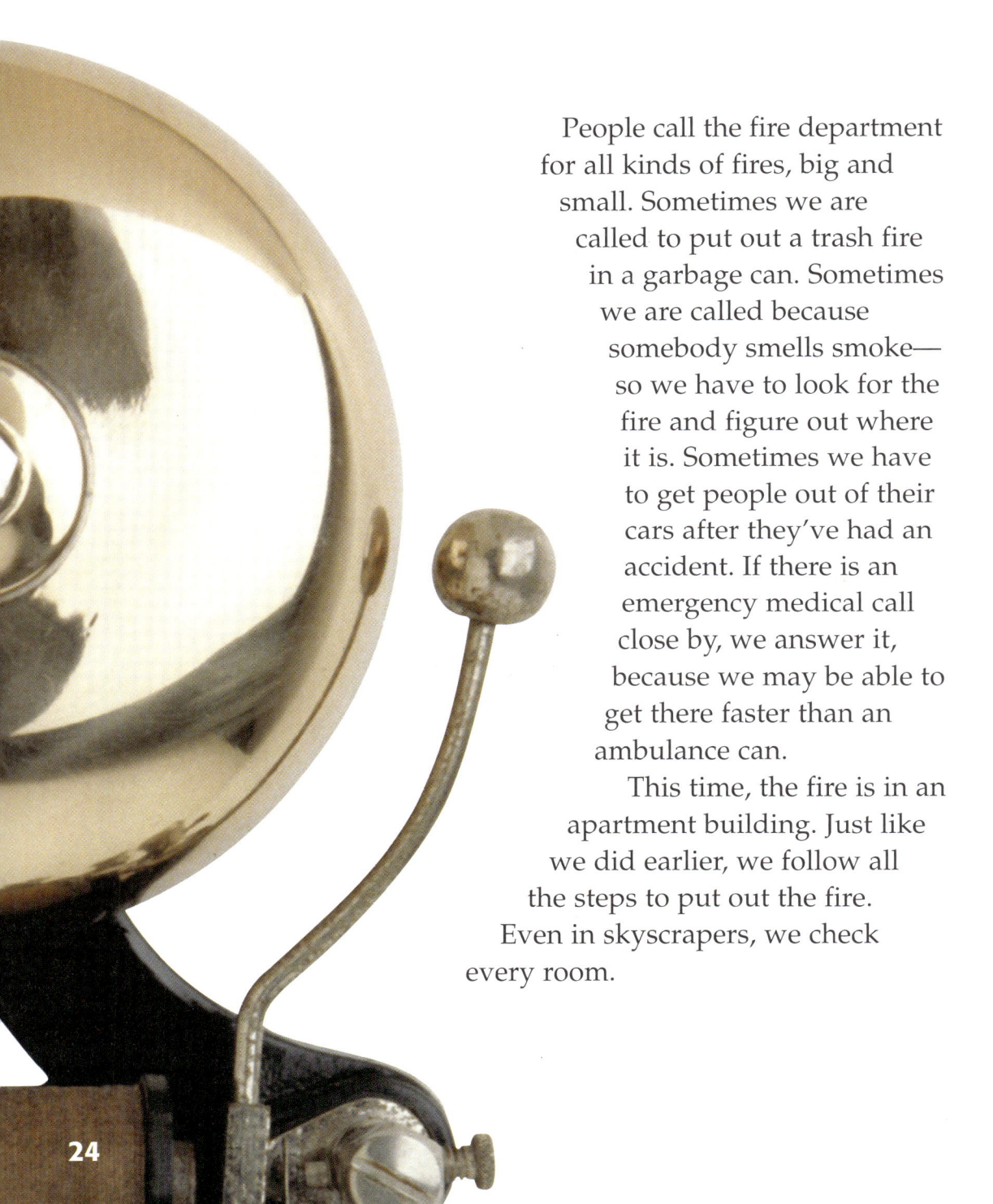

People call the fire department for all kinds of fires, big and small. Sometimes we are called to put out a trash fire in a garbage can. Sometimes we are called because somebody smells smoke—so we have to look for the fire and figure out where it is. Sometimes we have to get people out of their cars after they've had an accident. If there is an emergency medical call close by, we answer it, because we may be able to get there faster than an ambulance can.

This time, the fire is in an apartment building. Just like we did earlier, we follow all the steps to put out the fire. Even in skyscrapers, we check every room.

Smoke alarms in this building went off when the fire started. The smoke alarms warned everyone in time to escape. Every home should have smoke alarms!

Any time you hear the smoke alarm, you should leave your building quickly and quietly. Escape routes are the fastest and safest ways out of a place. This is a drawing of the building's escape routes. Do you see the big red X over the elevator? The elevator is not an escape route. You should never use an elevator during a fire. If the electricity goes out, you'd be trapped in a metal cage that could get hotter and hotter.

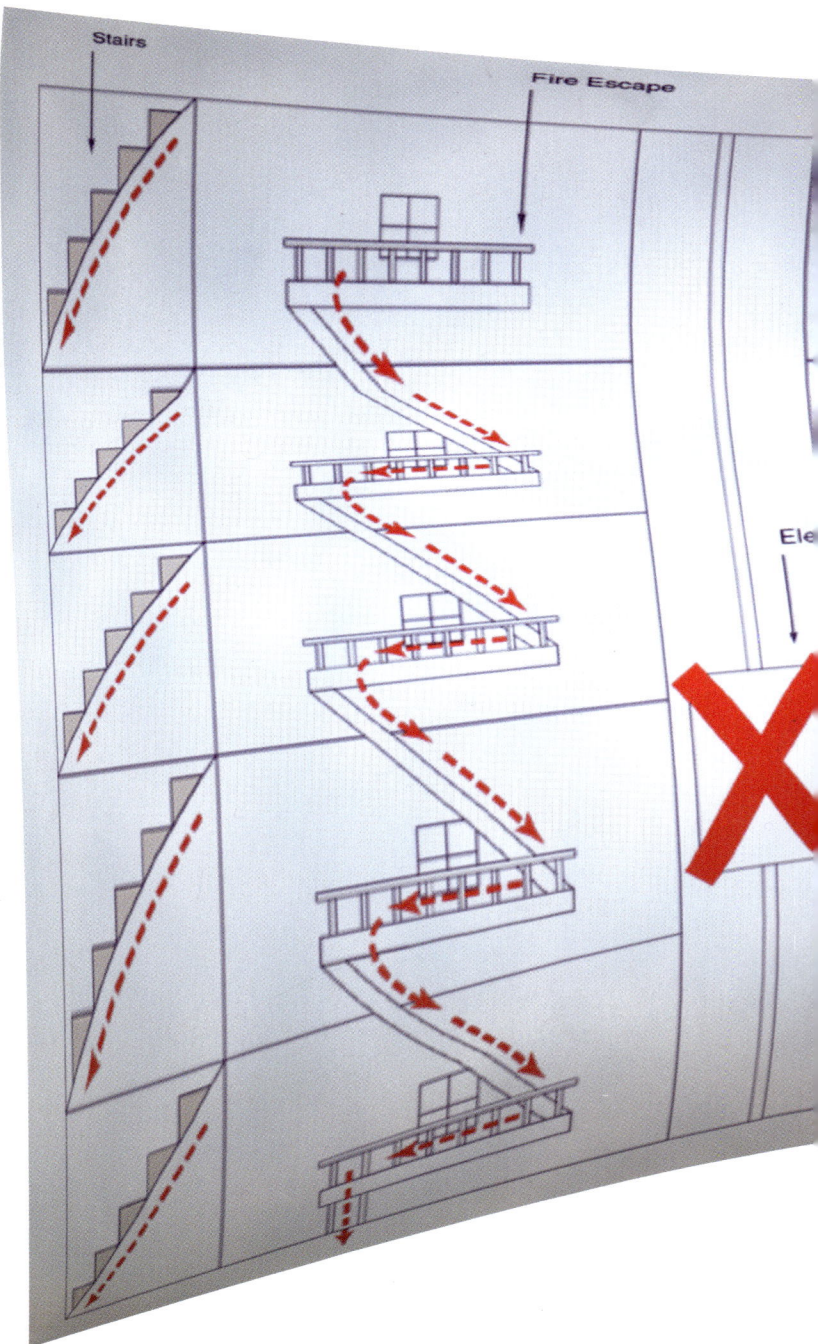

This building has two escape routes. One way to get out is to use the inside stairs. The other is to use a fire escape. A fire escape is a metal stairway attached to the outside of a building. Do you know why it's a good idea to have more than one escape route? If one way is blocked by fire, you can get out the other way. What are the escape routes in your home?

In this building, the fire was burning near the top floor. We could have run up the stairs with our hoses. But the fire was spreading too quickly. Running up the stairs would have taken too long.

Monica went up in the ladder truck. She turned on the ladder truck's hose and sprayed it on the fire. A couple of minutes later, the fire was out. Monica made it look easy. Her hard work and practice paid off.

Our hoses have three different kinds of nozzles that produce three different kinds of spray. One kind is like a water jet. Another kind is a stream of water—a stream can reach a fire that is farther away. Sometimes we use the nozzle that produces a misty fog. The fog can cool down a hot building by taking the heat out of the air.

Firefighters get a lot of help during a fire. James is a police officer. He helps to control traffic around the fire and keep crowds under control. Gwen is a paramedic. She helps take care of anyone who is injured during the fire. We all work together.

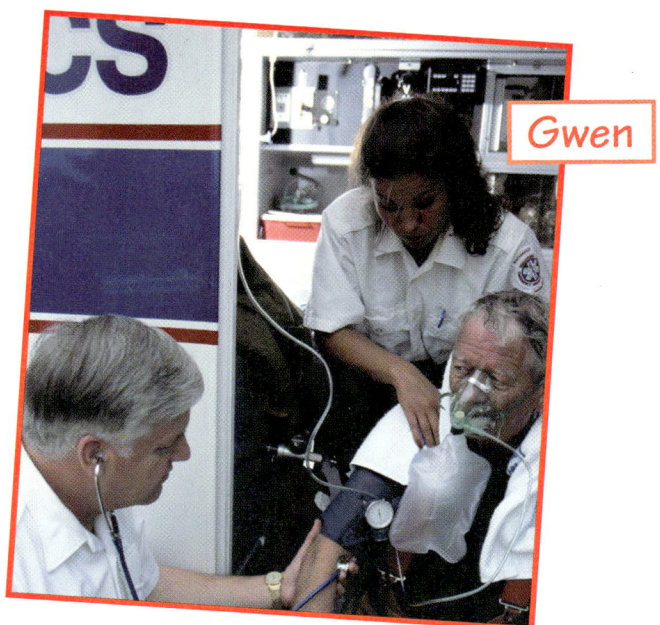

Gwen

James

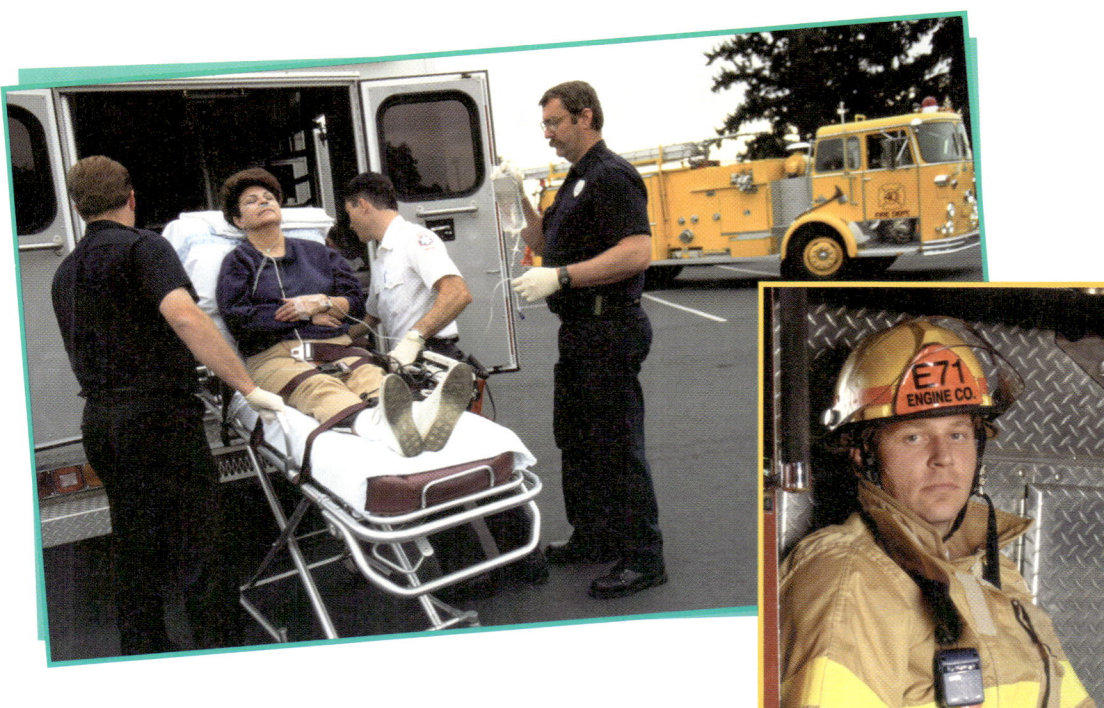

My job makes me feel good about myself. I save people's lives, homes, and businesses. It is a hard job, but it is the only job for me. How about you? Do you have what it takes to be a firefighter?

For Information About Becoming a Firefighter, Contact:
International Association of Fire Fighters
1750 New York Avenue, NW
Washington, DC 20006

National Fire Protection Association
Batterymarch Park
P.O. Box 9101
Quincy, MA 02269-9101

Firefighter Education, Training, and Requirements:
Requirements vary. In most areas, a firefighter must be at least 18 years old, have a high school diploma, and be in excellent physical condition. Some areas require firefighters to complete training at firefighter-training academies and other areas require firefighters to have a college degree from a two- or four-year program. Many fire departments also require firefighters to complete emergency medical technician (EMT) training. Most new firefighters serve a trial period that usually lasts from six months to a year. During this period, they receive a combination of classroom and hands-on training. They make sure that they want to become firefighters.

Related Careers:
Emergency Medical Technician (EMT)
Fire Inspector
Police Officer
Lifeguard
Park Ranger